W9-DAW-414

The Atom

by Elizabeth R. Cregan

Science Contributor
Sally Ride Science
Science Consultant
Jane Weir, Physicist

MISSION: SCIENCE

Sally Ride
Science

Sally Ride Science™ is an innovative content company dedicated to fueling young people's interests in science.

Our publications and programs provide opportunities for students and teachers to explore the captivating world of science—from astrobiology to zoology.

We bring science to life and show young people that science is creative, collaborative, fascinating, and fun.

To learn more, visit www.SallyRideScience.com

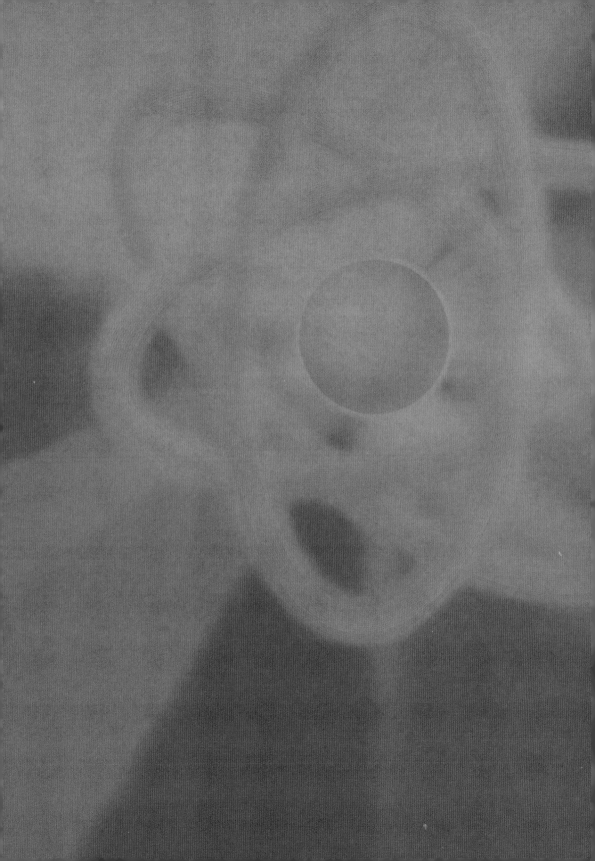

First hardcover edition published in 2009 by
Compass Point Books
151 Good Counsel Drive
P.O. Box 669
Mankato, MN 56002-0669

Editor: Mari Bolte
Designer: Heidi Thompson
Editorial Contributor: Sue Vander Hook

Art Director: LuAnn Ascheman-Adams
Creative Director: Keith Griffin
Editorial Director: Nick Healy
Managing Editor: Catherine Neitge

 This book was manufactured with paper containing at least 10 percent post-consumer waste.

Library of Congress Cataloging-in-Publication Data
Cregan, Elizabeth R.
The atom / by Elizabeth R. Cregan.
 p. cm. — (Mission: Science)
Includes index.
ISBN 978-0-7565-3953-5 (library binding)
1. Atoms—Juvenile literature. 2. Matter—Constitution—Juvenile literature.
3. Radioactivity—Juvenile literature. I. Title. II. Series.
QC173.16.C74 2008
539.7—dc22   2008007724

Visit Compass Point Books on the Internet at *www.compasspointbooks.com*
or e-mail your request to *custserv@compasspointbooks.com*

Table of Contents

Nature's Building Blocks

Your breakfast, your shoes, your hands, this book—they all have something in common. In fact, everything around you has one thing in common: it is all made of matter. Scientists say that matter is anything that takes up space. Even if the space is too small to see, matter is still there.

But what is matter made of? What is in that tiny world of particles that we usually cannot see? That unseen world is made up of atoms, the building blocks of matter. Atoms are everywhere—in your breakfast, in your shoes, in the tallest mountains, and in the largest oceans. They are the air you breathe, the things you touch, and the clothes you wear. Atoms make up the entire universe.

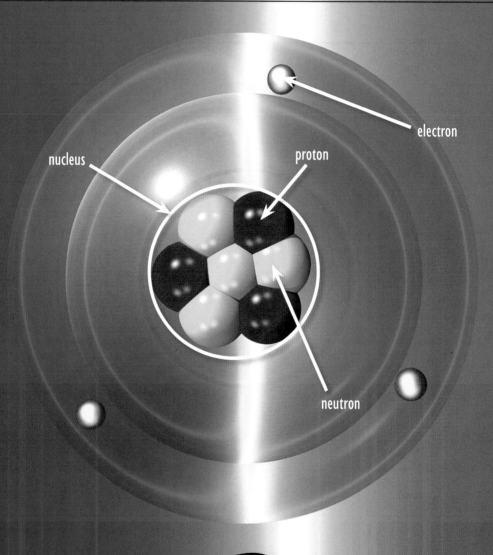

electron

nucleus

proton

neutron

Did You Know?

Atoms are so tiny that it takes more than 1 million of them lined up in a row to cover the width of a single strand of hair.

If you could peek inside an atom, you would see a lot of activity. First you might notice a small, tightly packed center called the nucleus. Inside the nucleus are even tinier particles called protons and neutrons. There is usually the same number of protons and neutrons in an atom. They squeeze together tightly to form the nucleus.

Look again, and you will see clouds of particles called electrons orbiting the nucleus. Each atom has the same number of electrons and protons. Electrons and protons have an electric charge. In protons, the charge is positive; electrons have a negative charge.

Together, they balance out the atom's charge, making the atom neither positive nor negative.

There are different kinds of atoms. Matter that is made up of just one kind of atom is called a chemical element. Oxygen, for example, is a chemical element because it has just one kind of atom. There are 94 natural chemical elements, each with its own type of atom.

Isotopes

Sometimes atoms that make up one element can have different numbers of neutrons. Each new version of the element is called an isotope.

"Light" elements usually have as many neutrons as protons; "heavy" elements usually have more neutrons. Atoms with not quite the right number of neutrons can exist for a while but are radioactive and unstable.

So, You Want to Be a Physicist?

If you're curious and creative, physics might be the field for you. Physics is the science of studying energy and matter and how the two behave and interact. Physicists try to answer both large and small questions about the universe by studying the natural world—from tiny particles to giant galaxies.

Physicists do experiments to try to answer these questions. They also teach and write about their experiments. Margaret Burbidge, a physicist, studies the stars. Her research has shown how heavier elements can be built from lighter ones inside stars. Her work is definitely out of this world!

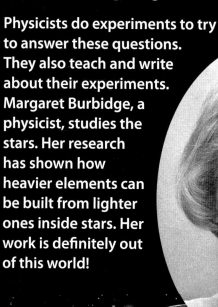

For a long time, scientists thought that protons, neutrons, and electrons were all the parts of an atom. Then they learned that there was more. Protons and neutrons are made of something even smaller—tiny particles called quarks.

Scientists have worked for more than 2,000 years to learn what we know about atoms. All that information is part of what is called the atomic theory. But scientists also realize that there is much more to learn about atoms. Now they wonder if quarks are made of even smaller particles. With more research and new equipment, perhaps they will find out. The study of atoms began in ancient Greece, but it is still going on today.

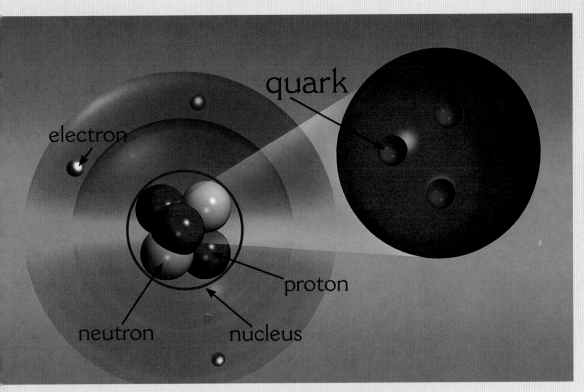

Protons, neutrons, and electrons are very tiny parts of an atom. In the 1960s, scientists found even tinier particles called quarks.

Old and New

Ancient Greek philosophers like Democritus and Aristotle observed the world around them and wondered how it worked. Many thought that all matter was made of four elements: air, fire, water, and earth.

Democritus questioned whether it was possible to break down matter into smaller pieces. He wondered if you could keep breaking it down into tinier particles forever. He decided that the answer to his question was no. At some point, he believed, there would be a pile of tiny bits that could no longer be broken down. He named those bits *atomos*, which means "not able to be divided."

▲ Democritus (c. 460 B.C.–c. 370 B.C.) believed that everything that exists now has always existed.

▲ Aristotle (384 B.C.–347 B.C.) was a brilliant philosopher and scientist

Aristotle, like Democritus, thought that matter was made up of four elements. And he believed there was a fifth element—ether—that filled up outer space. Aristotle also believed that heat could change one element into another. For thousands of years, people believed Aristotle's ideas. Scientists started a branch of science called alchemy. They tried to change metals such as lead into gold and silver. They experimented with elements such as mercury, lead, and sulfur. They also invented many tools that modern scientists still use, such as beakers, scales, and special pots for heating elements.

Did You Know?

Although the alchemists never figured out how to turn lead into gold, they did discover a new element—phosphorous. It was discovered when someone thought he could turn urine into gold because they were the same color. His work led to the discovery of phosphorous, which is used on the tips of matches.

John Dalton (1766–1844) is best known for his pioneering work in the development of the atomic theory.

Alchemy was used for thousands of years, and few thought much more about the old idea of atoms. But in the 1600s, scientists no longer relied on guesswork. They formed a hypothesis, or theory, and then tested it with experiments. By the 1800s, scientists had learned that elements do combine to form new substances. Water is a good example. Two atoms of hydrogen and one atom of oxygen combine to make water.

In the early 1800s, English scientist John Dalton took another look at the old Greek idea of atoms. He believed that matter was indeed made of atoms. Dalton also believed there were many kinds of atoms, and groups of one kind of atom make up an element. He found that all atoms of one element are the same.

Dalton also recognized that atoms have mass, which he called atomic weight. A basic unit of atomic weight came to be called a dalton, named after John Dalton, of course.

Dalton thought you could tell atoms apart by their atomic weights. He also thought atoms were the most basic units of matter and couldn't be divided any further.

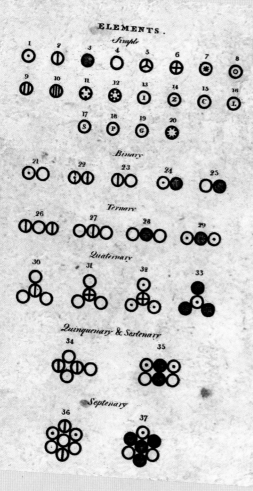

ELEMENTS.
Simple

John Dalton described elements and their combinations in his table of chemical elements.

Hydrogen

Scientists discovered that the simplest, or lightest, element, was hydrogen. They assigned it an atomic weight of one dalton. The weight of every other element is figured by comparing it to the atomic weight of hydrogen, the lightest atom.

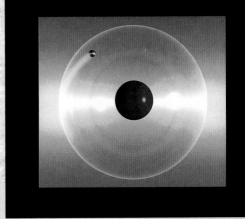

Scientists still had questions. Why are elements different? What makes them different? Is it possible to look inside an atom? Can two elements be combined? They would soon discover answers to some of their questions. And they would find that the alchemists weren't all wrong. Certain elements can combine to make what's called a compound. Rust is a good example of a compound. It is a combination of the atoms of iron and the atoms of oxygen. The compound is called iron oxide.

J.J. Thomson (1856–1940) was awarded the Nobel Prize in physics for his discovery of the electron in 1906.

In 1897, English scientist J.J. Thomson conducted several experiments that helped him discover electrons. First he made a glass tube that was empty of all air and gases—nearly a perfect vacuum. When he ran an electric current through the tube, he saw a special glow. The glow Thomson saw was energy. He called it cathode rays.

German scientists believed this glow was made by Aristotle's ether. French and English scientists thought it was caused by some kind of particle that glowed when hit by electricity. Thomson then proved that cathode rays were made of particles, which he named corpuscles.

Thomson believed that all atoms had corpuscles that were much smaller than the atom itself. Scientists would one day realize that Thomson's corpuscles were actually electrons that orbit the nucleus of an atom.

Most televisions, with the exception of LCD ➤ and plasma TVs, rely on cathode ray tubes to display images on the screen.

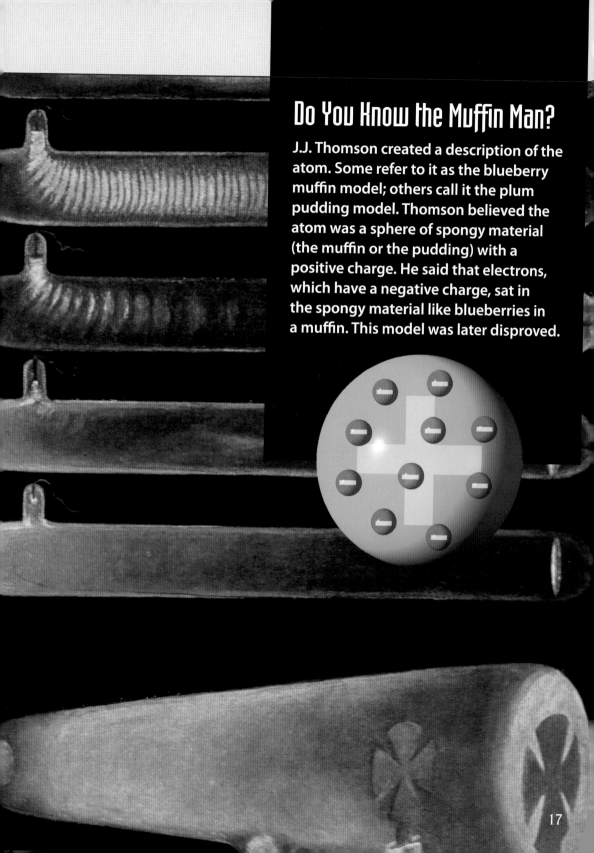

Do You Know the Muffin Man?

J.J. Thomson created a description of the atom. Some refer to it as the blueberry muffin model; others call it the plum pudding model. Thomson believed the atom was a sphere of spongy material (the muffin or the pudding) with a positive charge. He said that electrons, which have a negative charge, sat in the spongy material like blueberries in a muffin. This model was later disproved.

Other scientists studied the special glow that J.J. Thomson saw in his glass tube. They called this energy source X-rays. Thomson learned that corpuscles could expose film to take pictures. They could even expose film when the tube was wrapped in black cloth.

Scientists were curious about X-rays. One found that the element uranium gave off energy that was even stronger than X-rays.

Most scientists ignored this, but Polish/French scientist Marie Curie wanted to learn more about uranium and its energy. She and her husband, Pierre, tested many elements and found several that emitted powerful energy. Marie Curie named the energy radioactivity.

The Curies wondered where the energy came from. Something was happening inside the atom, something that held many mysteries.

Marie and Pierre Curie studied radioactivity in their laboratory in the late 1800s and early 1900s.

Destroying Cells

Marie and Pierre Curie handled radioactive materials for many years, which made them very ill. Their hands were always numb, and they lost weight. They realized that radiation from the elements they were researching was killing the cells in their bodies. However, they also realized that radiation could kill unhealthy cells as well, such as cancer cells. Today radiation is widely used as a cancer treatment.

18

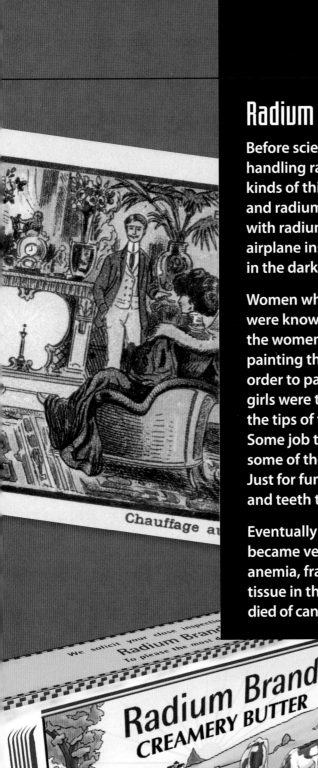

Radium Girls

Before scientists realized the dangers of handling radium, people used it for all kinds of things. There was radium butter and radium toothpaste. A paint made with radium was used on watches and airplane instruments to make them glow in the dark.

Women who worked with radium paint were known as "Radium Girls." Many of the women worked in watch factories, painting the numbers on watches. In order to paint the small numbers, the girls were taught to use their lips to keep the tips of the brushes pointy and clean. Some job trainers would even swallow some of the paint to show that it was safe. Just for fun, the girls painted their nails and teeth to make them glow in the dark.

Eventually many of the Radium Girls became very sick. Symptoms included anemia, fractured bones, and deadened tissue in the jaw. Hundreds of workers died of cancer caused by radium exposure.

Everyday products like makeup or butter often contained dangerous amounts of radium before scientists knew it was bad for your health.

Chauffage au

Radium Brand

Radium Brand
CREAMERY BUTTER

We solicit your close inspection
To please the most

Ernest Rutherford worked as J.J. Thomson's assistant and built upon his work. Rutherford was quite interested in X-rays and radioactivity. He studied the element uranium and exposed it to a strong magnetic field.

In this way, he discovered that it threw off particles that made radiation, or energy. He thought the atoms must be made of lots of these small particles.

To prove his theory, Rutherford shot particles at a thin piece of gold foil. It came to be called the Gold Foil Experiment.

▲ Ernest Rutherford (1871–1937), the father of nuclear physics

The Gold Foil Experiment led Rutherford to conclude that atoms contain a very small positive charge.

Rutherford found that most of the particles went through the foil, but some bounced back. The results made him believe that those particles bounced off of a dense core. He called it the nucleus. He believed that the rest of the atom was mostly empty space with electrons orbiting the nucleus.

Rutherford's experiment proved that Thomson's blueberry muffin model was wrong. The "blueberries" were flying around the muffin, not sitting inside of it. He also thought there might be a particle with no charge in the atom. Another scientist would discover this particle, called the neutron.

The Alchemists Weren't All Wrong

It's hard to imagine that people really believed it was possible to turn a metal like lead into gold or silver. Scientists worked for centuries trying to do just that. Along the way, they found some new elements, but no one ever turned lead into gold. As it turns out, they had the right idea. It was just backwards.

Today we know that radioactive elements such as radium decay and turn into lead. It just takes a little time—almost 20,000 years!

A New Model

In 1913, Danish scientist Niels Bohr made a new model of the atom. He worked with the ideas of Ernest Rutherford who found that electrons were revolving around the nucleus of an atom.

But Bohr went further and assigned each electron an orbit at a specific distance from the nucleus.

▲ Niels Bohr (1885–1962) was awarded the Nobel Prize in physics in 1922.

Did You Know?

Bohr and his son, Aage, are one of only six father-son pairs to have won the Nobel Prize. Aage followed in his father's footsteps by winning the Nobel Prize in physics in 1975.

The Right Time

German Scientist Maria Goeppert-Mayer (1906–1972) grew up during an exciting time. Modern physics was young and alive, and new theories were coming forward all the time. Many of her teachers were among the leading scientists of the day. In 1963, Goeppert-Mayer was awarded the Nobel Prize in physics for her research on the nucleus of an atom.

Bohr called the distances "energy levels." When an electron absorbs a unit of energy, called a quantum, it becomes excited and "jumps up" to a higher level.

Later physicists found that they cannot predict exactly what orbit an electron might be on at any given time. They can only estimate where it might be. Scientists also later found that electrons in orbit create a wave, something like the vibrations of a plucked guitar string.

◀ Bohr was the first scientist to apply the quantum theory to the study of physics. He created the Bohr model in 1915, which showed the most important molecular and atomic structures of an atom.

Atomic Comics

Work with radioactivity had a big effect on the entire world. Comic books like *Radioactive Man, Atomic Mouse, Atomic Rabbit, Inside the Atom, Reacto Man,* and *Atomic Superboy* were very popular in the 1950s and 1960s. Some were written to explain atomic energy and the use of electricity. Others told fantastic stories where radiation turned regular people into superheroes.

KA-BOOM

proton

free
neutron

ENERGY

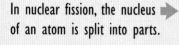

In nuclear fission, the nucleus of an atom is split into parts.

neutron

Irène Joliot-Curie was the daughter of Marie and Pierre Curie. For many years, she was her mother's assistant in the study of radioactivity. After her mother died, Joliot-Curie and her husband, Frédéric Joliot, continued researching radioactivity, specifically radioactive decay of elements. They searched for ways to make radioactive substances in the lab. They found that some substances decay in seconds, while others take millions of years.

Irène Joliot-Curie (1897–1956) and her husband, Frédéric Joliot (1900–1958), were awarded the Nobel Prize in chemistry in 1935 for their joint discovery of artificial radioactivity.

Their work led to the discovery of nuclear fission, or splitting apart the nucleus of an atom. For a very long time, scientists thought an atom could not be split. Eventually they found out that it is possible, but very hard to do. Splitting the atom of a heavy element such as uranium creates large amounts of energy. It is referred to as artificial radioactivity. Nuclear fission produces the explosion of nuclear weapons and produces energy for nuclear power plants.

In 1935, Irène and Frédéric shared the Nobel Prize in chemistry for their discovery of artificial radioactivity. Twenty years later, Irène died of cancer, just as her mother had. Working with radioactive materials caused their illnesses.

25

Atom Smashers

The more scientists studied the atom, the more complicated it seemed. They realized that there was much more to atoms than they thought. Huge machines called particle accelerators helped them find more subatomic parts, or tiny particles that are smaller than an atom. Physicists use particle accelerators to search for the tiniest building blocks of matter.

A particle accelerator covers acres of land. To see it all, you would need to view it from a helicopter. Particle accelerators are often called atom smashers, because that's what they do. They smash electrons into atoms at a high speed, breaking protons and neutrons into tinier pieces.

In an atom smasher, an electromagnet moves a beam of electrons down a copper tube at high speed. The largest atom smasher is the Large Hadron Collider in Switzerland. It uses 1,700 superconducting magnets and is more than 17 miles (27 km) long. When the electrons reach the end, they smash into an atom. Subatomic particles like quarks and radiation are released. Magnets, computers, and other equipment record what happens. These devices are called particle detectors.

With particle detectors, physicists have discovered that protons and neutrons have three quarks each. A powerful nuclear force called the strong force holds the quarks together. The strong force is what is responsible for the enormous explosion of an atomic bomb.

American physicist Murray Gell-Mann (1929–) received the 1969 Nobel Prize in physics for his research on quarks.

The Particle Zoo

In 1963, American scientist Murray Gell-Mann found that all subatomic particles are made of even tinier particles. He called them quarks, a name he picked from one of his favorite books. He found six types of quarks. He called them up, down, charm, strange, top, and bottom. Gell-Mann was only joking when he named the quarks, but somehow the names stuck.

Atom smashers have helped find hundreds of subatomic particles. There are so many that scientists call them the particle zoo.

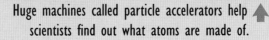

Huge machines called particle accelerators help ⬆
scientists find out what atoms are made of.

The Future for Atoms

Scientists continue to build more powerful atom smashers so they can find new subatomic particles. Perhaps they will even find particles that are smaller than a quark. Scientists still aren't sure that the quark is nature's smallest unit.

There may always be questions about atoms that scientists can't answer. But they aren't finished learning about the atom. Studying the atom has already led to many discoveries—X-rays, cancer treatments, atomic energy, artificial elements, atomic weapons, and more. And scientists continue to create new ways to use the information they already have.

Who knows what the future will hold?

X-rays are used to diagnose injuries and diseases in humans as well as animals.

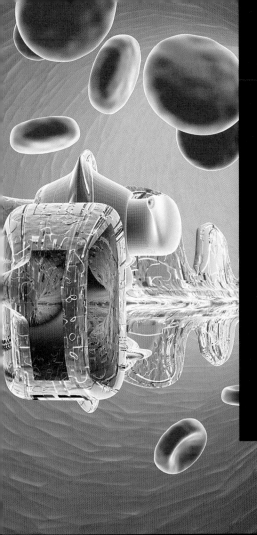

A Robot You Can Swallow

Imagine swallowing a robot so tiny it would take a microscope to see it. Scientists are working on ways to build very tiny objects called nanorobots. Nanorobots are built by arranging atoms one at a time.

In the future, it may be possible to program nanorobots to find cells in the human body that cause illnesses like cancer. These nanorobots would destroy the cancer cells and leave healthy cells alone. Doctors may even be able to send messages to nanorobots with sound waves to check how many cells they have destroyed.

Pioneers in atomic science often had to work with things that they could not see or touch themselves. They couldn't see atoms one at a time. Instead, they had to use indirect evidence. Indirect evidence is when you observe the effects of something. Then you make conclusions about the thing itself. It's like studying footprints in the mud to figure out who walked through the garden.

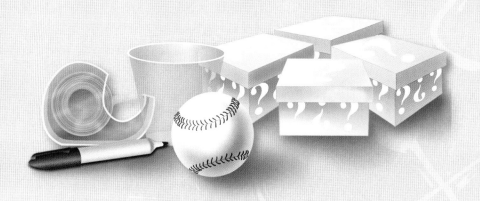

Materials

- empty boxes, labeled with letters or colors
- collection of ordinary classroom or household items
- scale
- table

Procedure

1   Ask someone else to prepare a number of mystery boxes. If you are doing this experiment in school, your teacher will prepare the boxes. In each mystery box there should be one or more items from your classroom or home. Each mystery box should weigh the same when empty.

2   Have whoever prepared the mystery boxes write down the items they used. You will match the items in the boxes to the items on this list.

3 Without opening the mystery boxes, try to figure out what is inside each one. You can use your list as well as any scientific instruments, such as a scale, you have available.

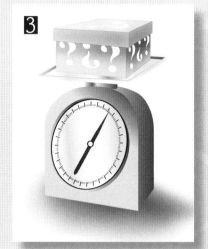

4 Record which items you think are in which boxes (hypothesis) and the reasons for your hypothesis for each mystery box.

5 Open the boxes and see if you were right.

Glossary

alchemy—early chemistry that did not use the scientific method

atom—smallest particle of an element

atomic theory—theory that proposes that matter is made up of atoms

atomic weight—combined weight of an atom's protons and neutrons

cathode rays—beams of electrons

electricity—flow or stream of charged particles, such as electrons

electron—negatively charged particle that whirls around the nucleus of an atom

element—substance that cannot be broken down into simpler substances

fission—splitting apart of the nucleus of an atom to create large amounts of energy

isotope—atoms that have the same number of protons but different numbers of neutrons in the nucleus

mass—amount of matter a substance contains

matter—particles of which everything in the universe is made

neutron—particle in the nucleus of an atom that has no electric charge

nucleus—dense core of an atom that contains protons and neutrons

particle—small piece of matter

particle accelerator—machines that speed up subatomic particles to near the speed of light and use them to smash into and break apart atoms for study

proton—positively charged particle in the nucleus of an atom

quantum—unit of energy

quark—tiny particles that make up protons and neutrons

radioactive decay—giving off of subatomic particles by an atom

radioactive—being made up of atoms with nuclei that can break apart

radium—radioactive element

subatomic particles—pieces that are smaller than and part of an atom

uranium—radioactive element found in pitchblende and used in nuclear power stations

vacuum—space that is completely empty of all matter, including air and other gases

X-rays—powerful images taken with cathode rays

Antoine Henri Becquerel (1852–1908)
French physicist who discovered radioactivity by accident in 1896 when a piece of uranium left in a dark desk drawer made an image on photographic plates; won the Nobel Prize, along with the Curies, in 1903

Niels Bohr (1885–1962)
Danish physicist who received the Nobel Prize in physics in 1922 for his contribution to understanding the structure of atoms that are made up of protons, neutrons, and electrons

Marie Sklodowska Curie (1867–1934)
Polish/French physicist who was awarded two Nobel Prizes (1903 and 1911) for her pioneering work in radioactivity

Pierre Curie (1859–1906)
French physicist who shared the Nobel Prize with his wife, Marie Curie, in 1903 for their research on radiation

John Dalton (1766–1844)
English chemist and physicist best known for developing the atomic theory

Albert Einstein (1879–1955)
German physicist best known for his theory of relativity and specifically mass-energy equivalence ($E = mc^2$)

Maria Goeppert-Mayer (1906–1972)
American physicist known for her research on the nucleus of an atom; received the Nobel Prize in physics in 1963, becoming the second woman to receive the award (Marie Curie was the first)

Irène Joliot-Curie (1897–1956)
French chemist and daughter of Marie and Pierre Curie, who together with her husband, Frédéric Joliot, received the Nobel Prize in chemistry in 1935 for the discovery of artificial radioactivity

Dimitri Ivanovich Mendeleev (1834–1907)
Russian chemist credited with creating the first version of the Periodic Table of the Elements

Wilhelm Conrad Röntgen (1845–1923)
German physicist who discovered X-rays in 1895

Ernest Rutherford (1871–1937)
English physicist who studied the element uranium and became known as the father of nuclear physics

Joseph John Thomson (1856–1940)
English physicist known for the blueberry muffin model and the discoveries of the electron and isotopes; received the Nobel Prize in physics in 1906

450 B.C. Leucippus introduces the idea of atoms as individual units of matter

430 B.C. Democritus claims that the atom is the simplest form of matter, is invisible, and cannot be destroyed

1704 A.D. Isaac Newton suggests a mechanical universe with small solid masses in motion

1803 John Dalton's atomic theory decares that each element has a particular kind of atom; he also argues that all of an element's atoms have the same mass and properties

1869 Dimitri Mendeleev arranges elements into seven groups with similar properties; publishes the first Periodic Table of the Elements

1874 G.J. Stoney suggests that electricity is made of negative particles called electrons

1887 J.J. Thomson discovers cathode rays

1895 German physicist Wilhelm Röntgen discovers X-rays

1896 Henri Becquerel discovers radioactivity

1898 Marie Sklodowska Curie and her husband, Pierre, study uranium and thorium and call the spontaneous decay "radioactivity"; they also discover two elements: polonium and radium.

1900 German physicist Friedrich Dorn discovers the element radon

1906 Hans Geiger develops an electrical device that makes a clicking sound when hit with alpha particles

1907	Ernest Rutherford finds that atoms have a small nucleus orbited by electrons
1913	Niels Bohr assigns each electron an orbit at a specific distance from the nucleus
1914	H.G.J. Mosely organizes elements in the periodic table by their atomic number—the number of protons in the nucelus
1929	Scientists make the earliest particle accelerators that break apart atoms
1932	James Chadwick discovers the neutron, which is in an atom's nucleus and has no electrical charge
1935	Irène Joliot-Curie and Frédéric Joliot share the Nobel Prize in chemistry for their discovery of artificial radioactivity
1938	Scientists find that heavy elements capture neutrons and form unstable products that undergo fission
1942	Enrico Fermi conducts the first controlled chain reaction, releasing energy from the nucleus of an atom
1963	Murray Gell-Mann discovers that all subatomic particles are made up of even tinier particles called quarks
1982	A single atom of element 109 is produced in a German laboratory
2008	The Hubble Space Telescope discovers methane and water, the molecules necessary to form and sustain life, on an extrasolar planet

Additional Resources

Gore, Bryson. *Physics: A Hair Is Wider Than a Million Atoms.* Mankato, Minn.: Stargazer Books, 2006.

Juettner, Bonnie. *Molecules.* Farmington Hills, Mich.: Kidhaven Press, 2005.

Solway, Andrew. *A History of Super Science.* Chicago: Raintree, 2006.

Stewart, Melissa. *Atoms.* Minneapolis: Compass Point Books, 2003.

Stille, Darlene R. *Atoms & Molecules: Building Blocks of the Universe.* Minneapolis: Compass Point Books, 2007.

Woodford, Chris, and Martin Clowes. *Atoms and Molecules.* San Diego: Blackbirch Press, 2004.

On the Web

For more information on this topic, use FactHound.

1. Go to *www.facthound.com*

2. Type in this book ID: 0756539536

3. Click on the *Fetch It* button.

FactHound will find the best Web sites for you.

Elizabeth R. Cregan

Elizabeth Cregan is a freelance writer living in Jamestown, Rhode Island. She enjoys writing about a wide variety of topics for children and young adults including science, natural history, current events, and biography. She has a bachelor's degree in special education and a master's degree in distance education. She is also the owner of Cregan Associates, a consulting firm specializing in grant and technical writing for state government human services information technology clients.

Image Credits